CHEMICAL DEPENDENCE AND RECOVERY
A Family Affair

Revised Edition

JOHNSON INSTITUTE®

Other booklets in this series are:

Alcoholism: A Treatable Disease

Chemical Dependence: Yes, You Can Do Something

Detachment vs. Intervention: Is There a Conflict?

Detachment: The Art of Letting Go While Living with an
    Alcoholic, *Evelyn Leite*

The Dynamics of Addiction, *George A. Mann, M.D.*

The Family Enablers

How It Feels to Be Chemically Dependent, *Evelyn Leite*

Recovery of Chemically Dependent Families

What You Need to Know about Blackouts, *Lucy Barry Robe*

Why Haven't I Been Able to Help?

INTRODUCTION

We all grow up thinking we know what a family is and how it functions. So when someone in our family becomes dependent on alcohol or some other drug, we think we *ought* to know what to do. Actually, most people don't. But they can learn. This booklet is meant to help you understand what's really happening to the chemically dependent person, what's happening to you (someone close to that person), and what's happening to the whole family.

We've all heard about alcoholism and drug addiction, but some of us might not know the term *chemical dependence*. Before discussing it, we need to make it clear that alcohol is a drug just as much as cocaine, marijuana, heroin, "uppers," and "downers" are. Over the years, experts in treating chemically dependent persons have learned that no matter which drug one is dependent on, the disease--and it truly is a disease--is basically the same. We can recognize it by basically the same symptoms, and the ways of recovering from it are basically the same.

All mood-altering chemicals have one effect: to change the mood, the feelings, of the person who uses the chemical. Chemical dependence, then, refers to a harmful dependence on *any* mood-altering drug, alcohol and others alike. If we sometimes focus our attention on alcohol and alcoholism in this and other booklets, it's only because so many people know them and their effects firsthand.

What we want to emphasize in this booklet is that chemical dependence of any member of the family is a *family* disease, not just a disease in that individual, for the family is inevitably affected and involved in many important and harmful ways. However, as we'll point out, this disease can be arrested, and all members of the family can be restored to live healthy, happy lives.

Editor's Note: To avoid endless repetition of "he or she," we've usually settled for the commoner "he." But keep in mind the real situation: many women are chemically dependent. For instance, in the United States about 40% of alcoholics are women.

3

By inquiring what you can do about chemical dependence in your family, you've already made a good start. Keep up the good work. And remember--help *is* available for you, for the chemically dependent person you love, and for your whole family.

THE FAMILY SYSTEM
AND CHEMICAL DEPENDENCE:
AN OVERVIEW

No two families are alike. Yet all families have some traits in common; there's a kind of *family system* at work. For instance, we've learned that all families tend to react in patterned, predictable ways when a family member becomes chemically dependent whether on alcohol or on any other drug. Understanding this family system will help you understand what happens when chemical dependence strikes a family.

First, what is a family? It's those people--traditionally a mother, a father, and some children--who depend on one another for meeting their social, emotional, spiritual, and physical needs. "Family" could be extended to include others who become family members through birth, marriage, legal adoption, or in less formal ways such as participating in family functions, lending support during troubled times, or sharing in other family activities.

Each family member is somehow a part of every family activity and situation. Each one somehow experiences the pains, joys, and successes of the whole family and of each person in it. And the family as a whole is touched by events in a way that non-family members can never experience.

"What goes on" in a family might be charted this way:

Dysfunctional---Nurturing

At one end of the line is a *nurturing* atmosphere: not necessarily problem-free, but a situation in which family members love and like one another, respect one another's qualities and capabilities,

4

and accept one another's shortcomings. The members trust and support one another, and the family is relatively happy and emotionally secure.

At the other end of the line is a *dysfunctional* atmosphere--one in which the family system functions abnormally. In that situation, there are big problems that cause family members much pain and insecurity. Family members often show their pain and insecurity by such negative behavior as inappropriate anger, aloofness, resentment--and sometimes very clearly through chemical dependence.

Every family system can be graphed on the line that moves between a nurturing atmosphere and a dysfunctional one. Every family is somewhere on this continuum at any given time, and the family can move in either direction as a result of events that occur in the system. Moreover, *the family tends to move as a group*, not as unrelated individuals.

When a family system is healthy, all the members are able to feel a full range of emotions, and they feel free to express their emotions to one another. They don't avoid conflict or problems at any cost: differences can be talked over. Individuality is accepted, and family members listen to one another. Every person's mistakes are a least tolerated, but each person is held responsible for his or her own behavior. The members of this family system are able to face stress and pain as they work through their problems and their differences. In this open and supportive system, all the members have high self-esteem, respect for one another, energy, and love.

When a family member becomes chemically dependent, however, the family begins to move toward the dysfunctional end of the continuum. In this booklet we'll call the family with a chemically dependent member a "chemically dependent family," and we'll look closely at the dysfunction that such a family is apt to undergo and what family members can do to restore the family to health and happiness.

Chemical dependence--alcoholism or other drug dependence--is a disease that may start with one person, but eventually it involves *every* member of the family. (How this happens will be explained later.) This involvement in turn makes it possible, in a sense, for the chemical dependence to continue--indeed, to grow worse. Sometimes the chemical dependence will develop in other family members. Even apart from actual chemical dependence, though, the emotional life in a chemically dependent family is almost certain to become less healthy. Every member of a chemically dependent family inadvertently plays a part in this malfunction, and each family member requires help in breaking this destructive pattern. Unless there's a constructive interruption--technically called an *intervention*--each person's negative patterns will continue, and the children in the family will carry their negative patterns into new family systems as they mature, marry, and have children of their own.

Living in a constantly shifting, distressing family and not daring to talk about that situation is a difficult, emotionally painful experience for all family members. The family experiences fear, anger, loneliness, hurt, guilt, and shame as the disease progresses, and typically the family members themselves unwittingly and literally become part of the problem. In short, chemical dependence becomes a family illness. Many professionals refer to this family illness as co-dependence (more on that later).

To protect themselves against the painful feelings resulting from chemical dependence, family members develop defenses that help them meet their emotional needs. Their occasional defensive behavior at the beginning of the dependence grows into a steady defensive posture as the family disease of chemical dependence progresses. There are several stages in each member's progression into dysfunction. Not all family members will be in the same stage at the same time. But as the disease of the chemically dependent person progresses, family members typically go through the following four stages:

1. They'll experiment with defensive behaviors that aren't healthy for them or helpful to the family.

2. Their practice of defensive behaviors will lead them to seek refuge in the most comfortable of the three general defensive behavior patterns available to them (these will be discussed later in this booklet).

3. Unfortunately, practice makes perfect; they'll become habituated to their defensive roles and will suffer all the harmful consequences these roles bring upon them.

4. They'll lose hope for family change and look for a way to escape from their pain.

STAGES OF CHEMICAL DEPENDENCE IN THE INDIVIDUAL

To understand the idea of the "chemically dependent family," we need to understand the disease process of chemical dependence and the effects of this disease on the chemically dependent individual. At the Johnson Institute, chemical dependence is often referred to as the "feeling disease," because it progressively affects the emotional life of the chemically dependent person. All persons operate within a certain range of emotions. These emotions range from the feeling of euphoria, involving highest elation or well-being, to a feeling of deep, pronounced emotional pain. Pain includes such feelings as anger, sadness, loneliness, fear, depression, and low self-worth. Between these extremes are the "normal feelings" or "even keel" feelings of everyday life that make people say, "I feel fine" or "I'm okay."

Most persons live in the area between euphoria and pain most of their lives. They work at being contented, but the stresses and joys of life create mood swings toward pain or toward euphoria.

Once a person has entered the early stage of chemical dependence, alcohol and/or other drugs generally produce progressive, harmful emotional changes that make the dependent person and the people closest to him increasingly dysfunctional. For the dependent person, the progression of dependence generally has four phases: the Learning Phase, the Seeking Phase, the Harmful Dependence Phase, and the Using-to-Feel-Normal Phase.

THE LEARNING PHASE

In this phase the person is introduced to the chemical and discovers its power. He learns that the chemical can produce a mood swing, usually toward euphoria, as the Feeling Chart below shows. This mood swing is positive, pleasant, rewarding; and most important, it's without any emotional cost, consequences, or pain. At this stage, the person sees no reason to forgo further experimentation with chemicals. Chemicals seem reliable; they make him feel good. After the chemical effect wears off, the person returns to his normal living. Learning at this stage is experimental, but it has a marked influence on the new user.

```
Pain                    Normal Feelings                    Euphoria
                   |x------------------------>|x
----------------------------------------------------------------------------
                   <--------------------------Return to Normal
```

THE SEEKING PHASE

This phase refers to how the person relates the newfound effects of the mood-changing chemical to his *social* life--for instance, parties, business luncheons, entertaining his friends. The person uses the chemical more frequently and in a great variety of social situations, but he does observe some self-imposed rules. He confines his use to appropriate occasions (e.g., parties, family gatherings), times (e.g., he never drinks before 5 p.m.), and amounts (e.g., never more than three drinks). Using the chemical still moves the person toward euphoria, and he returns predictably (except for possible occasional hangovers) to normal after stopping the use.

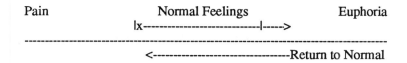

```
Pain              Normal Feelings              Euphoria
            |x--------------------------|----->
-----------------------------------------------------------------------------------------
            <---------------------------------Return to Normal
```

"Social drinkers" remain in this phase. But victims of chemical dependence progress to Harmful Dependence.

THE HARMFUL DEPENDENCE PHASE

This third phase occurs when the person using the chemical becomes harmfully dependent on it to achieve the state of euphoria. Why only some people progress from the Seeking Phase to Harmful Dependence we don't know. What we do know, though, is how the dependent person's behavior changes in this stage. He begins to suffer real losses in his life because of chemical use.

By now he's probably been using the chemical for some time. Furthermore, it has probably caused some family problems, and everyone in the family has tried to solve those problems. But nothing has worked; things have steadily become more painful.

As dependence grows, the dependent person's behavior usually changes. He might throw overboard long-held moral and family values. He might use abusive language or take a punch at his spouse or a child. Whatever the change is, family members know "something's wrong," because his behavior has changed markedly. Of course, judging what's "wrong" will vary from family to family, depending on the family's values.

This change in behavior affects the dependent person as well: the more he sees how his conduct conflicts with his long-held values, the more his negative feelings about himself grow.

In this Harmful Dependence Phase, the dependent person begins to experience loss of control over the chemical use. He can no longer predict how he's going to act, how many drinks he's going to have,

9

or what the outcomes of a drinking episode are going to be. The result of the usage is no longer a predictable return to normal; rather, the loss of control ends in a return to pain. Notice on the chart how the feelings change.

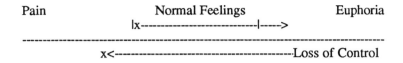

Pain   Normal Feelings   Euphoria

In an attempt to cope with the emotional pain, the dependent person begins to look forward to using the chemical again. He becomes preoccupied with using it and with the resulting euphoric feelings. Unfortunately, further use and out-of-control behavior produce more pain--pain that only increases anticipation of relief from pain by further use of the chemical.

Anticipation and preoccupation change the dependent's life-style. True, he establishes and observes specific times for chemical use--e.g., he drinks only at noon and before supper. But he sets these times not to limit his drinking, but rather to ensure that there are regular opportunities for chemical use. Interruptions or delays of the established pattern create anxiety in him, and he usually meets them with angry resistance. He now regularly breaks the rules established for "social use" in the Seeking Phase. Now he must have a supply of the chemical on hand, and as his tolerance for it increases so that he needs more of it to create the desired feelings, he develops ingenious ways of getting, using, and hiding it.

The dependent's whole life now revolves around the chemical, and his life deteriorates as health, spirituality, emotional stability, and interpersonal relationships become adversely affected. Growing emotional stress, anxiety, pain, and self-hatred are suppressed, medicated with chemicals, and blamed on others.

The dependent person "helps" himself in strange ways. Protective defensive behavior and memory distortion resulting from chemical use provide at least some emotional relief. Dependence brings about a growing self-delusion that won't allow him to see that his chemical use has anything to do with what others see as his changing, deteriorating behavior. In fact, he doesn't even realize that his behavior contradicts his long-held values.

The vicious circle of compulsive chemical use produces unpredictable behavior, and the unpredictable behavior results in an increase of negative feelings that he smooths over with more chemicals. If he continues to drink or use other drugs, he'll move toward the fourth phase, that of using chemicals to feel normal. In this phase, continued alcohol and/or drug use can lead to serious physical deterioration and even death.

THE USING-TO-FEEL-NORMAL PHASE

In this phase the dependent person uses chemicals to reach what he remembers as normal feelings, rather than to attain a feeling of euphoria, which is beyond his reach in this stage. What he's actually trying to do is medicate himself against the chronic emotional pain, depression, and anxiety he constantly experiences except when intoxicated. During this stage, the drinking or other drug use may at best result in brief periods of emotional relief, but this relief is little more than the absence of pain. Deterioration continues in all areas of his life.

Pain   Normal Feelings   Euphoria

        Chronic Anxiety and Depression
xxx------------------------>x
---------------------------|-------------------------------|------------------------
Delusion<----------

Anger

Projections

The disease of chemical dependence is fatal. If the dependence isn't arrested, the person will die prematurely.

STAGES OF CHEMICAL DEPENDENCE IN THE FAMILY

The family members progress in their illness in a series of stages very similar to those that the dependent person goes through. Before we discuss those phases, however, it will be useful to discuss the particular feelings manifested in each of the phases and the ways those feelings come out in the members of the family. We'll then briefly investigate three general behavioral patterns that family members use in coping with their own problems and with the chemically dependent person.

FAMILY FEELINGS AND WAYS OF SHOWING THEM

Chemical dependence, especially in its later stages, is stressful for all members of the family. As dependence progresses in any one member of the family, all members experience certain emotions. Though they may not talk openly about anger, guilt, shame, hurt, fear, and loneliness, they do experience all these feelings. Family members need to learn that they're neither bad nor abnormal if they have these feelings. They also need to learn how to express these feelings appropriately and how to fulfill their own emotional needs.

Anger

Among family members, anger can often be explained as a love/hate relationship. Family members love the dependent person, but they hate the painful experiences that everyone goes through because of his chemical dependence. The painful experiences bring about anger and resentment toward him, and it's not easy to separate the dependence from the person.

Shame

During some of the painful experiences resulting from the dependent person's use of alcohol or drugs, the family has felt ashamed of him. As the situation in the family becomes worse, shame grows to include being ashamed of the whole family--the dependent, the other members of the family, and even oneself. Shame produces feelings of low self-worth in each member of the family.

Guilt

The family members begin to blame themselves and one another for the painful experiences they're having. Each family member may secretly feel that somehow he or she is responsible for the drinking and that "if only I could change," everything would be all right. Such self-blame produces more feelings of guilt and shame.

Hurt

Emotional pain can be broad and deep. It's painful to see a loved one deteriorate as chemical dependence progresses. It hurts to become involved in arguments or to witness angry exchanges between members of the family. Many times the dependent blames others for his alcohol of drug use. Messages such as "If you wouldn't nag, I wouldn't drink" or "You want to know why I drink? Look in the mirror" cause deep emotional hurt and deepen feelings of guilt and shame.

Fear

Living in a constantly shifting, distressed family produces fear: fear of arguments, fear of financial problems, fear about the dependent's usage, fear that the dependent will get drunk, or even fear that everything will remain the way it is. And there's fear of the future: what will happen to the family if things keep getting worse? The fears compound proportionately with the internalized emotional stress each family member already feels.

Loneliness

The stressful family situation results in a breakdown of normal, rewarding family communication. Family love and concern are lost in the stress and crises of day-to-day living. The isolation created by the lack of nurturing communication in the dependent family results in more loneliness for everyone.

DEFENSIVE BEHAVIOR OF FAMILY MEMBERS

To protect themselves from further emotional pain and to hide the emotions they're experiencing but don't want to admit, family members begin to take on protective defensive behavior. At the Johnson Institute, we speak about three generalized categories of defensive behavior an individual can adopt in a stressful dependent family situation: being too good to be true, being rebellious, and being apathetic.

Being Too Good to Be True

This defensive behavior disguises the pain of the individual and of the family. Being "too good" gives the illusion that the family has no problem. When an individual is being "too good," he's looking for reward that being good may bring. He's also looking for rewards that are just not available in a dysfunctional family--rewards such as recognition, praise, special family treatment, and more responsibility. Beyond the matter of rewards is the hope that the "being-too-good" behavior will somehow bring about a positive change in the chemically dependent person's behavior. Children often think, "If I'm good enough, maybe Mom and Dad won't have to drink so much."

Being "too good" includes exaggerated behavior such as

- achieving for the family: in school, at work, in sports, in the community;

- doing more than one's share around the house;

- counseling the family, patching up family fights and relationships;

- being cute and funny at inappropriate times; entertaining to relieve stressful situations;

- struggling for perfection, not allowing for any mistakes, denying mistakes;

- intellectualizing: acknowledging family stress and pain only on a thinking level; denying feelings about stress;

- parenting: children acting as parents, disciplining other children, worrying about family finances; adults acting as parents to other adults;

- meeting everyone's expectations, trying to keep everyone happy;

- being rigidly obedient, *always* following *all* the rules.

What's unhelpful about "being too good"? While admirable in some ways, this behavior insulates the chemically dependent person from having to experience the harmful consequences of this dependence. To insulate or protect the chemically dependent person is to *enable*, because doing what the dependent person ought to be doing or covering up for him enables the dependence to continue.

Being Rebellious

Some family members react to chemical dependence with their own kind of misbehavior. The effect is to remove the spotlight from the behavior of the chemically dependent person. By being rebellious and acting out, a family member draws attention away from the primary family problem of the dependence. Most often, a rebellious family member receives negative recognition--i.e., blame for the family stress. There's a payoff for the rebellious person, however. Being rebellious is effective in disguising pain, and such behavior rewards the rebellious individual with family attention, even though it's negative.

Rebellious behavior may involve

- being dishonest;

- being late for work;

- acting out in school and at home;

- breaking house rules;

- defying authority at home or on the job;

- starting arguments with neighbors;

- bullying, playing hurtful pranks;

- bossing the neighbor's children;

- rejecting the family: developing a "family" of friends of whom the parents wouldn't approve;

- neglecting one's children or becoming abusive.

Being Apathetic

This defensive behavior disguises a person's pain and provides relief for the apathetic person and the family. It's difficult to describe this passive, defensive behavior because the apathetic or passive person does very little, shows little emotion, takes no action that's not absolutely necessary. Passive behavior is manifested in the many ways in which the person quietly withdraws from frightening, stressful, or painful situations in a dependent family. Rewards for being apathetic are contained in feelings of safety and self-pity. What's seen as calmness and a philosophical attitude toward trouble is really rigid, deliberately unfeeling behavior. Being apathetic isn't the same as a healthy "I-don't-care" attitude. On the surface, apathy often looks like serenity and acceptance.

But the apathetic person simply refuses to see the problem and its effects on the whole family. While the apathetic person may appear calm, his behavior doesn't quiet the turmoil and anxiety he feels inside.

Being apathetic is often indicated in the following ways:

- withdrawnness;

- habitual quietness;

- separateness from others;

- passive rejection of the family;

- fantasy, daydreaming;

- passive rejection of relationships, inside or outside the family.

The apathetic family member actually enables the disease to progress. By refusing to confront the disease, by not recognizing the problem for what it is, he helps maintain the illusion that nothing is out of order in the family.

THE FOUR STAGES OF
FAMILY CO-DEPENDENCE

Now let's turn to the four phases of the illness of family members who aren't chemically dependent. Helping professionals commonly refer to the illness of family members of chemical dependents as "co-dependence." Co-dependence is the consistent pattern of traits and behaviors recognizable in individual family members that can result in physical, emotional, mental, or social dysfunction often as severe as that of the chemically dependent family member. First of all, it may seem strange to hear that the family members who aren't alcoholic or otherwise drug dependent have an illness. But once we look at the behavior that family members use in coping with the chemically dependent person, it won't seem strange at all to call their behavior and accompanying emotional states ill or at the very least "dis-eased." Family members can become just as abnormal in their behavior, just as emotionally mixed up, just as self-destructive as the dependent person. For simplicity's sake, we'll use the term "co-dependent" to refer to non-chemically-dependent family members.

Remember that these phases can begin at different times for different members of the family. While it's likely that family members will progress through the phases at approximately the same time, they don't necessarily do so. Few family members, in fact, begin their own illness process until the chemically dependent person is far down the line into his dependence. Usually family members won't show signs of thir co-dependence until the dependent person has begun the Harmful Dependence Phase. When he enters this phase, the family has a need to develop its own protective defensive behaviors. Let's look at these family phases.

The Learning Phase

The first phase, as with the chemically dependent individual, is the Learning Phase. The process of harmful dependence takes some time before it becomes an observable problem for a family. As the disease process develops, everyone in the family knows that stress is present and that family life is changing. The stress may show itself in increasing arguments, tension, less communication, or strained spousal and parent/child relationships. In an attempt to protect themselves and bring back family stability, family members experiment with the three forms of defensive behavior (being too good, being rebellious, or being apathetic). As they try these different ways of coping with the developing "chemically dependent family" experience, they're learning what defensive behavior works best for them in times of crises and stress. Although this learning may not be a conscious experience, it's a strong and habit-forming one.

18

The Seeking Phase

In this phase the family tries to discover what the problem is and how to solve it. In the Learning Phase there's no awareness that drinking or other drug use is the problem In the Seeking Phase there are hints--flashes of awareness--that *maybe* drug use is the problem. Family members may even mention this idea to one another. However, the thought is quickly rationalized away and replaced by the false hope that it's really not the problem. This process is called family denial.

In time, the evidence is too clear to ignore. As family members recognize, however sketchily, that alcoholism or other drug dependence is a problem in their family, individual family members use defensive behavior in a manipulative way. They consciously choose what helps them live their lives most smoothly: being too good, being rebellious, or being apathetic.

A rather serious problem for the family members at this point is that they sincerely believe they can control the dependent person's chemical use by manipulating the family environment. Being more loving, achieving, acting out, blaming, being angry, or withdrawing from the dependent person can all be ways of trying to manipulate or control his chemical use. This sincere belief that the family can control the chemical use is called family delusion. The hard fact is, though, that neither manipulation nor defensive behavior by the family can control either the alcohol or other drug use or the chemically dependent individual.

Denial and delusion on the part of the family enable the chemically dependent family member to move farther and deeper into the self-destructive dependence. The family members may not be reacting much differently to the chemically dependent person than they did when they first noticed problems, but a major change has been made in the whole situation. The chemical dependence is now recognized, at least by the co-dependent family members.

Early on, their reactions to the chemically dependent person were random and experimental. They really didn't know what the problem was. Now they do, even if only vaguely. By continuing to practice their acquired styles of coping with the chemically dependent person, they may be helping themselves feel better temporarily, but in the long run their own unhealthy co-dependent behavior will catch up with them and turn them into angry, resentful, emotionally impaired persons.

The Harmful Phase

In this phase the family's defensive behavior becomes compulsive. Their reactive behavior becomes just as predictable and automatic as that of the dependent person. It's at this point that the co-dependent traits and behaviors of individual family members often become fixed and rigid as members try to control the chemically dependent family member. The family becomes locked into its defensive behaviors (being too good, being rebellious, or being apathetic), and the behaviors become roles: being too good becomes "the Good Kid"; being rebellious becomes "the Family Rebel"; and being apathetic becomes "the Passive Adult" or "the Withdrawn Child." Because of the stress and repeated use of these defensive behaviors, the defenses become habitual roles for the family members.

In this Harmful Phase no one confronts the dependent person about his compulsive use of chemicals. Rather, the family blames that person just as if he had freely chosen to be dependent and had knowingly caused all the problems. The family illness of co-dependence grows more and more rigid. Family members rightly feel helpless to control the chemical use, but they become so deluded that they often begin to believe that they and their behavior caused the dependence in the first place.

The resulting feelings of guilt, shame, and self-blame add to the family members' feelings of isolation and loneliness. In order to cope with growing pain, family members unwittingly build a denial system around it. As strange as it may seem, if asked about their emotional pain, most family members would think they were being truthful when they responded that everything was all right. Effectively denying the pain, each individual accepts the defensive, painful, dependent family life-style as normal. Only when this life-style becomes undeniably painful will individuals begin to look for a way out.

The Escape Phase

This is the final phase of the family disease process. It's marked by repeated major crises; financial problems, work problems, physical, emotional, and social problems become routine occurrences. Family members who have suffered overpowering feelings of guilt, rage, and disloyalty regarding the chemically dependent member begin to act on their bad feelings and seriously begin to search and find ways to escape. Separation and even desertion can occur during this phase, and, worst of all, suicide is sometimes chosen as a way of ending the problems.

Family members do arrive at the point where they feel emotionally exhausted, unable to cope any longer, and numbed by a false sense of guilt. Walking away from the situation seems to be the last, the best, and sometimes the only way to survive or to find peace.

If the co-dependent family member has reached this point, however, separation from the situation doesn't eliminate the painful emotions, the protective, defensive life-style, or the resentments that have grown up in the family. By now, each individual in the family needs some kind of personal help if he or she is ever to return to a happy, healthy life-style.*

* For more information about the family illness of co-dependence, read *Diagnosing and Treating Co-dependence: A Guide to Professionals Who Work with Chemical Dependents, Their Spouses and Children*, by Timmen L. Cermak, M.D., published by the Johnson Institute.

THE PRIMARY CO-DEPENDENT

As surprising as it might seem, chemical dependence involves a cooperative effort between at least two people. When a person is chemically dependent, at least one other person is involved in a way that literally enables the chemical dependence to continue and become even worse. At the Institute we call this person a primary co-dependent. More often than not, all family members are co-dependents to some extent, usually because they don't realize the effect their behavior is having on the chemically dependent person. Among the family co-dependent members, though, one person usually stands out.

In a family situation, the chemically dependent person usually--in an unplanned, unnoticed way--develops an important primary enabling relationship with one other member. In a marriage, this other enabling person is usually the spouse. The primary co-dependent may, however, be in any relationship to the chemically dependent person: he or she may be a child, a parent, another relative, a work supervisor, a family friend. The primary co-dependent attempts to protect both the chemically dependent person and the other family members from the negative effects of the alcoholism or other drug dependence.

It's important to keep in mind that the primary co-dependent begins enabling with good intentions: wanting to care for another person, wanting to help someone "with a problem." Under normal circumstances, helping someone handle a problem is a loving thing to do. If one's spouse was feeling ill, one would say, "Go to bed; you shouldn't be working. I'll call work and tell them you're sick." But suppose a wife knew her spouse had a drinking problem and was sick because he'd had too much to drink the night before. And suppose this had happened frequently. If a wife called then, she wouldn't really be helping; she'd be covering up the real problem by lying about "the flu" and by encouraging him not to see that drinking was interfering with his work.

Enabling starts out with small, simple tasks that the primary co-dependent takes over for the dependent person. The primary co-dependent may find the dependent person irresponsible with money matters, but instead of confronting him about irresponsibility or the necessity of contributing toward family expenses, he makes all the payments just to avoid an argument. Once again the primary co-dependent would be enabling the chemically dependent person to be irresponsible. What makes enabling destructive is that the chemically dependent individual doesn't have to face any consequences of his chemical use. So the illness continues because he's not forced to see the harm he's causing.

The other co-dependent family members take their cues from the primary co-dependent and thus indirectly give that person even more than ordinary authority in the family. Many times the primary co-dependent takes on the role of both parents, making all decisions, picking up the pieces after a fight, and trying to maintain the illusion that everything in the family is fine. Enabling can be done so well by the primary co-dependent that the dependent person and outsiders can really believe that the chemically dependent person has everything in order in his life. But this situation can't go on forever. The growing needs of the dependent call for ever more covering up and support from the primary co-dependent. Eventually the primary co-dependent has to give up his other concerns and own needs to take care of the chemically dependent person. Matters arrive at such a state that whereas the primary co-dependent may have been receiving good feelings of self-worth from many different aspects of life, now he finds feelings of importance primarily from being needed by the dependent.

The chemically dependent person becomes the primary co-dependent's addiction much as chemicals have become the dependent person's addiction. On the one hand the primary co-dependent feels needed and important, but on the other hand he feels a growing resentment because of the burden of taking care of the dependent person. The primary co-dependent is compulsively driven and becomes unable to see how he's reacting to the dependent person.

Co-dependents become deluded; they suppress hurt, loneliness, and anger by keeping busy, and they devote an extraordinary share of their lives to the chemically dependent person.

The primary co-dependent often develops self-destructive behaviors: e.g., over- or under-eating, joining the dependent person in using chemicals, becoming indifferent to personal appearance, becoming ill from not taking care of himself. And the worst can happen: hate may take over where once there was love. Even then, in spite of all the prices paid, the primary co-dependent remains locked in to the dependent person, unable to see other choices for dealing with the situation, and he gains his only good feelings from taking care of the dependent person. Resentment becomes the primary co-dependent's poison just as the chemical is that of the dependent person. Normal human feelings are deadened, and the primary co-dependent may become hardened, cold, and bitter, with a feeling of being trapped, a feeling of hopelessness and despair.

FAMILY INTERVENTION

Contrary to the myth, not all chemically dependent people drink or use alike, nor do they all behave in the same way, drunk or sober. Some alcoholics drink daily; others are "binge" drinkers and stay "dry" for a time between binges. Some drink large amounts of alcohol; others consume relatively small amounts. For some, alcoholism appears early in life; for others, it appears after years of apparent "social drinking."

Some people develop problems with other drugs. For instance, millions of people across the country are dependent on cocaine, and that number keeps growing at a startling rate. Alarming numbers of teenagers and young adults have become dependent on marijuana, amphetamines (uppers), or illicitly obtained barbiturates (downers). Less well known but no less serious is the problem of the person who has used tranquilizers, sedatives, or "diet pills" under a doctor's prescription to a point where harmful dependence has developed. Such persons aren't likely to recognize chemical dependence in themselves, and, unfortunately, many families won't easily recognize it either. In chemical dependence, denial is almost always present: "I don't have a problem," or "I can quit any time I want to."

LOSS OF CONTROL

One of the common features of all chemical dependence is loss of control. Truly dependent persons generally can't stay away from alcohol or the other drug for very long. Once they start using it, they can't stop. Some will drink or use moderately for a while without any harmful consequences. But if they're really chemically dependent, they won't be moderate for long, and when the family eases up its pressure, they increase the use.

WHAT IS INTERVENTION?

What can the family do once they suspect chemical dependence as the cause of family problems? They can begin a process known as intervention. Note that intervention is a process, not a single event. It's a *process* by which the harmful, progressive, destructive effects of chemical dependence are interrupted and the person receives some kind of constructive help in ending the use of mood-altering chemicals and in developing new, healthier ways of coping with his needs and problems. There's a shorter, simpler way to define intervention: *presenting reality in a receivable way to a person out of touch with it.*

Intervention in chemical dependence is the most helpful, most supportive act the family can offer--and the sooner the better. It makes no sense (contrary to what was once thought) to let the victim "hit bottom" as a physical or emotional wreck before we offer help.

Families quite understandably hesitate about beginning the intervention process, because they fear things might get worse or feel that the person is beyond all help. And some family members are so resentful and angry that they have no desire to help the chemically dependent person. But these family attitudes can be changed.

PRINCIPLES OF INTERVENTION

Remember that intervention is a process, not a single event. It may take a long time after the opening intervention before the dependent person takes positive, appropriate action. But whatever the timing, certain things must happen in intervention. At the Johnson Institute we call them the five principles of intervention.

1. The important persons in the life of the chemically dependent person should be involved in the intervention.This includes all the immediate-family members, possibly the employer or work supervisor, and close friends if they have firsthand knowledge of the person's behavior and chemical use.

2. All these important persons should write down specific data about events and behavior involving the dependent person's use of chemicals.

3. They should then tell the chemically dependent person how they feel about what has been happening in his and their interrelated lives, and they give their information in a loving, nonjudgemental way.

4. Choices for help such as joining Alcoholics Anonymous, Cocaine Anonymous, Narcotics Anonymous, going to treatment, or seeking one-to-one counseling should be offered to the dependent person. If the person absolutely refuses all of these choices, the people involved in the intervention must insist that he answer the

26

question "What happens if you can't quit using the chemical?" They should make a firm and clear commitment to what their response will be if the person resumes chemical use. It's helpful to try to reach an agreement with the person that if he begins to use alcohol or other mood-altering substances again, he will then seek help.

5.   If the person agrees to seek help immediately, the family should see to it that professional help is available.*

HOW INTERVENTION BENEFITS THE FAMILY

An intervention process is as beneficial for the family as it is for the chemically dependent person. First of all, the family openly breaks its silence about the issue of chemical dependence. Each member can talk freely and honestly about his or her own feelings. A counselor who understands the process of intervention can give much valuable information about the family disease of chemical dependence. The family members can learn that they too have become part of the illness process. Now that they're open and honest about the problem and about their own feelings, they can give one another the support they need. The intervention process restores the family to a unity it hasn't experienced for a long time.

Education about the family illness of chemical dependence is one of the best means of preventing active chemical dependence in other members of the family. After the intervention, it's entirely possible--and happens very frequently--that members of the family besides the one who's the center of attention decide that they too have problems with chemical abuse.

*For more detailed information about the intervention process, read Dr. Vernon E. Johnson's latest book, *Intervention: How to Help Someone Who Doesn't Want Help, A Step-by-Step Guide for Families and Friends of Chemically Dependent Persons,* published by the Johnson Institute.

The enabling behavior that the family has been providing the chemically dependent person may be stopped, or it may be recognized for what it is, and the chances are that with this recognition the behavior will at least be reduced.

Family members will be made aware of the many different support groups available to them, and they'll be encouraged to attend one or other of these groups to take care of their own problems.

Finally, the chemically dependent person will know in his heart of hearts that his family genuinely cares about him, that they're willing to risk many things, even their relationship with him, to see to it that he knows the truth about the situation and has the opportunity to take advantage of any help available. Our long experience has shown that when an intervention is conducted with careful planning, preparation, and professional help, it's a highly effective means of involving the chemically dependent person and his family in a treatment and recovery program.

TREATMENT AND RECOVERY

Treatment for chemical dependence generally has two major thrusts: interrupting the use of any mood-altering chemical, and confronting the defensive behaviors that help maintain the dependence. The chemically dependent person must stop all chemical use if treatment is to be effective, because chemical use has become the center of the problem. The person must learn that he or she *can* get along without the chemical, whatever it is. It's also necessary to begin to change the dependent person's defensive behaviors, because the old defenses almost always lead back to chemical use and certainly don't fill the person's genuine emotional needs.

Examination of these defenses in treatment allows the person to become aware that these coping behaviors have not only failed to produce the desired results but have helped maintain and deepen the chemical dependence. Likewise, the dependent person must examine the needs that underlie the defenses; counselors and group therapy are very helpful in this examination. Once the needs have been identified, it becomes possible for the person to look at new behavior that can bring productive results.

In treatment for chemical dependence, the dependent person has some opportunity to discover and test new behavior and to experience the unfamiliar comfort that can be achieved when the stress of conflict--both from within and from the family--is lessened. Learning new behaviors that fill one's needs begins in treatment and continues through aftercare and then through regular participation in Alcoholics Anonymous, Cocaine Anonymous, Narcotics Anonymous, or other comparable groups for chemical dependents.

Because the need for treatment for the chemically dependent person is so desperately evident and is generally beneficial for the whole family, the fact that the family also needs treatment for its own problems is easily overlooked. At the outset, when talking about treatment for the family, it's important to dispel certain misconceptions. First, the family doesn't undergo treatment for the sake of the chemically dependent person. Second, the sobriety of the chemically dependent person doesn't depend on the rehabilitation of the chemically dependent family. Third, family recovery doesn't depend on the future sobriety of the chemically dependent family member.

When we talk about family recovery, the point is this: because chemical dependence develops into a family illness, virtually all members of the family need some kind of help toward recovery. Furthermore, if the chemical dependence has existed in the family over a long time, it's very likely that most members of the family will have developed harmful co-dependent traits or behaviors and will need some kind of outside help in restoring themselves to a state of health and happiness. For the family, this usually means a program of family care, individual counseling, and regular, active involvement in Al-Anon, Alateen, Adult Children of Alcoholics, or comparable self-help groups.

Why must a family have a program for recovery? Families who've lived with chemical dependence for a long time are usually so close to it that they can't begin to realize the scope of the problem. In their efforts to protect themselves from the pain and ravages of the disease of chemical dependence, they've developed their own limiting and emotionally insufficient ways of coping with the problem and have gradually slipped into an emotionally crippled life. Although their problems originated around someone else's chemical use, those problems won't necessarily go away even if that person begins to recover.

The best-known method of family care, and certainly the most easily accessible for people all over the United States, is active participation in the organization known as Al-Anon and in its junior counterpart, Alateen. These two organizations were founded to provide group support and a program for living that would help people recover from the problems they suffer from living with a chemically dependent person. Al-Anon and Alateen members follow a program almost identical to that of Alcoholics Anonymous, and they operate on confidentiality and self-help group principles. For more information about Al-Anon or Alateen, consult your local telephone directory.

A more recent development in self-help is the Adult Children of Alcoholics groups that have sprung up across the United States. These groups specialize in offering group support for adult children of alcoholics--children who usually no longer live with a chemically dependent parent or family member but who still suffer the crippling effects of having been raised in a chemically dependent family. For more information, call or write: The National Association for Children of Alcoholics (NACoA), 11426 Rockville Pike, Suite 100, Rockville, MD 20852; (301) 468-0985.

Families of chemically dependent persons tend to have problems that are very similar to the ones the chemically dependent person has. Families need to break through their own denial systems.

They too must learn that chemicals are the focus of the problem; and they need to realize that each person in a chemically dependent family is responsible for his or her own behavior.

Families sometimes have a very difficult task in breaking through the denial and delusion that have grown up around the chemically dependent family. They must somehow learn that while they're not responsible for all the problems in the family, they're indeed responsible for their own feelings and their own recovery. For family members, breaking through denial and delusion means that they discover that they have choices on how to behave, that their enabling behavior didn't and won't help the dependent person give up the chemical use, and that enabling behavior won't help them fill their own emotional needs.

Like the chemically dependent member of the family, other members of the family must learn that they have choices regarding their behavior; they can try out new behaviors and search for ways to fulfill their legitimate emotional needs.

Most persons raised in a chemically dependent family have never developed the ability to experience a full range of feelings. Recovering the rich and rewarding feeling of life that's part and parcel of the healthy family system may take a long time.

Whatever time it takes, recovery is worth the effort. And the chief point of this booklet is worth repeating: chemical dependence and recovery are a family affair.